**U.S. HISTORY Need to Know**

SilverTip

# The Dust Bowl

by Karen Latchana Kenney
Consultant: Caitlin Krieck
Social Studies Teacher and Instructional Coach
The Lab School of Washington

BEARPORT
PUBLISHING

Minneapolis, Minnesota

## Credits

Cover and title page, © Everett Collection/Shutterstock; 5, © Everett Collection/Shutterstock; 7, © LC-USZ62-103452/Library of Congress; 8–9, © LC-DIG-fsa-8b28546/Library of Congress; 11, © LC-DIG-fsa-8b32409/Library of Congress; 12–13, © Lanevskyi/Shutterstock; 15, © LC-DIG-ds-01322/Library of Congress; 17, © LC-USF34-016962-E/Library of Congress; 19, © Keith Corrigan/Alamy; 21, © World History Archive/Alamy; 22–23, © bruev/Getty Images; 25, © LC-USF33-030398-M5/Library of Congress; 27, © instamatics/iStock; and 29, © Jacky Co/Shutterstock.

## Bearport Publishing Company Product Development Team

President: Jen Jenson; Director of Product Development: Spencer Brinker; Managing Editor: Allison Juda; Associate Editor: Naomi Reich; Associate Editor: Tiana Tran; Senior Designer: Colin O'Dea; Associate Designer: Elena Klinkner; Associate Designer Kayla Eggert; Product Development Specialist: Anita Stasson

A NOTE FROM THE PUBLISHER: Some of the historic photos in this book have been colorized to help readers have a more meaningful and rich experience. The color results are not intended to depict actual historical detail.

*Library of Congress Cataloging-in-Publication Data*

Names: Kenney, Karen Latchana, author.
Title: The Dust Bowl / by Karen Latchana Kenney.
Description: Minneapolis, Minnesota : Bearport Publishing, [2024] | Series: U.S. history : need to know | Includes bibliographical references and index.
Identifiers: LCCN 2023005418 (print) | LCCN 20230C5419 (ebook) | ISBN 9798888220313 (hardcover) | ISBN 9798888222225 (paperback) | ISBN 9798888223468 (ebook)
Subjects: LCSH: New Deal, 1933-1939–Juvenile literature. | Dust storms–Great Plains–History–20th century–Juvenile literature. | Droughts–Great Plains–History–20th century–Juvenile literature. | Agriculture–Great Plains–History–20th century–Juvenile literature. | Great Plains–Social conditions–20th century–Juvenile literature. | New Deal, 1933-1939–Juvenile literature.
Classification: LCC F595 .K36 2024  (print) | LCC F595  (ebook) | DDC 973.917–dc23/eng/20230216
LC record available at https://lccn.loc.gov/2023005418
LC ebook record available at https://lccn.loc.gov/2023005419

Copyright © 2024 Bearport Publishing Company. All rights reserved. No part of this publication may be reproduced in whole or in part, stored in any retrieval system, or transmitted in any form or by any means, electronic, mechanical, photocopying, recording, or otherwise, without written permission from the publisher.

For more information, write to Bearport Publishing, 5357 Penn Avenue South, Minneapolis, MN 55419.

# Contents

Surviving the Storm . . . . . . . . . . . . . 4
New Farmers . . . . . . . . . . . . . . . . . . 6
Wheat Is the Way . . . . . . . . . . . . . 10
Black Blizzards . . . . . . . . . . . . . . . 12
The Great Depression . . . . . . . . . 16
Mass Movement . . . . . . . . . . . . . . 18
A New Deal for Farming . . . . . . . . 20
Back to Farming . . . . . . . . . . . . . . 24
The Future of Farming . . . . . . . . . 26

Grasses and the Soil . . . . . . . . . . . .28
SilverTips for Success . . . . . . . . . . .29
Glossary . . . . . . . . . . . . . . . . . . . . .30
Read More . . . . . . . . . . . . . . . . . . .31
Learn More Online . . . . . . . . . . . . .31
Index . . . . . . . . . . . . . . . . . . . . . . . .32
About the Author . . . . . . . . . . . . . .32

# Surviving the Storm

A massive black cloud took over the sky. People raced for cover as dust swept toward them.

On Black Sunday, the bright day was plunged into darkness by a huge **dust storm**. These kinds of storms raged across the **Great Plains** during the Dust Bowl. Why did they happen?

April 14, 1935, started out as a beautiful, sunny day. Then, the wind picked up. The sky turned dark as the storm came through. The day became known as Black Sunday.

# New Farmers

Before European **settlers** came, much of the Great Plains of North America was **grasslands**. This land west of the Mississippi River and east of the Rocky Mountains was healthy.

Then, the government made a law called the Homestead Act of 1862. Many settlers moved to the plains to become farmers.

> The Homestead Act gave land to settlers for free. Settlers had to agree to live on and work the land for five years. They also had to build on the land.

Settlers grew crops and raised cattle.

Unfortunately, many settlers didn't know how to farm grasslands. They plowed the grasses. This made the soil loose so their crops could grow, but it harmed the land.

Grasses have long, webbed roots. They add **nutrients** to the soil. Their roots also hold soil together and slow **erosion**.

Before settlers came, Native Americans lived on the Great Plains. They planted small farms and did not plow their fields. They also regularly changed where they planted crops so their nutrients could spread.

# Wheat Is the Way

In the 1920s, wheat from Europe became very expensive. So, many farmers across the plains started growing the crop. Wheat was making them lots of money.

Farmers kept planting more and more. This meant they were plowing up even more land.

European settlers brought wheat with them when they first came to North America. Many people used flour made from wheat to bake bread.

# Black Blizzards

When a severe **drought** started in 1930, the soil went from bad to worse. The ground dried out and crops began to die. The loose, dry soil had nothing to hold it down. When harsh winds blew across the plains, they swept the soil up. Soon, dust clouds darkened the skies.

Trees can block wind. They slow down the wind's speed. However, grasslands do not have many trees. Wind quickly swept across the Great Plains during the 1930s.

People called these storms black blizzards. The dust storms left behind huge dunes. Dust came into people's homes through windows and cracks.

The people on the plains did everything they could to block dust from their eyes and lungs. Still, many got sick from breathing the dust. Some even died.

> People tried many things to stop the dust. They wore masks. Some hung wet sheets from their windows. This trapped some of the dust before it could get inside.

**Drifted dust buried some farms and fields.**

# The Great Depression

The clouds of dust made life hard on the plains. But, the country's failing **economy** made everything worse. The Great Depression had started in 1929. Many people lost their jobs. They could not buy food. As a result, wheat prices went down. Farmers got less money for their crops.

> Animal life on the plains suffered during the drought, too. Locusts and rabbits couldn't find food. So, they turned to farms. The animals ate the few plants left in the fields.

# Mass Movement

For many, the drought and crop failure made it too hard to keep farming. By 1934, more than 35 million acres of land could not be farmed.

Families packed up what little they had. They left their farms and went west, looking for work.

Many former farmers didn't have money. They went west without a place to stay when they arrived. While they looked for work, they often lived in tents or shacks made from wood, cardboard, and metal.

# A New Deal for Farming

President Franklin D. Roosevelt knew farmers and other Americans needed help. So, he made a plan. It was called the New Deal.

Some New Deal programs helped raise the price of crops. Parts of the New Deal taught farmers how to take care of the land.

> Roosevelt's New Deal programs included more than just help for farms. They gave many Americans jobs. The New Deal set up systems to protect people's money in banks.

Some New Deal programs focused on planting trees. Workers made long rows of trees along the grasslands of the plains. These lines of trees stretched from North Dakota down to northern Texas. They helped block winds. This prevented soil from being lifted up in the future.

The government realized regrowing natural grassland was important, too. They bought land in the plains. Workers replanted grasses and other grassland plants. This held the soil in place. It added nutrients back into the ground.

These trees can still be seen today.

# Back to Farming

By 1938, the government programs were working. They had stopped more than half of the soil from blowing away.

Then in 1939, rain started falling again. The drought had ended by 1941. Farmers could begin farming again. This time, they worked to protect the soil on their lands.

> Soon after the Dust Bowl ended, World War II (1939–1945) started. America joined the fight in 1941. Wheat prices went up because of the war. So, farmers were paid more for their crops.

# The Future of Farming

Since the Dust Bowl, farmers have taken action to stop extreme dust storms. There are **restored** grasslands and better ways to protect the soil while farming. The plains are much healthier than they were in 1930. These effects will help protect farms and the soil into the future.

In the 1950s, another drought came to the Great Plains. However, farmers had learned from the Dust Bowl. This drought did not create the dust storms seen in the 1930s.

# Grasses and the Soil

Learn how grasses and their roots help keep the soil healthy on grasslands.

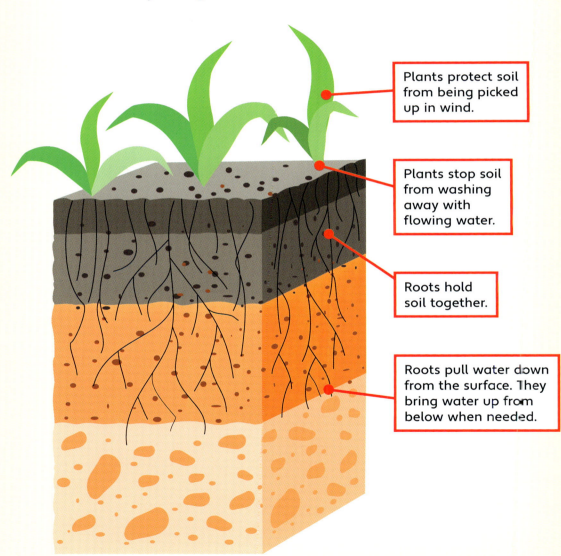

Plants protect soil from being picked up in wind.

Plants stop soil from washing away with flowing water.

Roots hold soil together.

Roots pull water down from the surface. They bring water up from below when needed.

# SilverTips for SUCCESS

## ★ SilverTips for REVIEW

Review what you've learned. Use the text to help you.

### Define key terms

drought
dust storms
Great Depression
Great Plains
New Deal

### Check for understanding

Explain how the way settlers farmed harmed the soil.

What did people do during the Dust Bowl?

How did the New Deal help turn around farming on the Great Plains?

### Think deeper

What do you think the Dust Bowl taught us? Do you think another Dust Bowl could happen in the future?

## ★ SilverTips on TEST-TAKING

- **Make a study plan.** Ask your teacher what the test is going to cover. Then, set aside time to study a little bit every day.

- **Read all the questions carefully.** Be sure you know what is being asked.

- **Skip any questions** you don't know how to answer right away. Mark them and come back later if you have time.

# Glossary

**drought** a very long period of time when there is less rain than normal

**dust storm** a large cloud of dusty soil that moves through the air and blocks sunlight

**economy** the system of buying, selling, making things, and managing money in a place

**erosion** the wearing away of rocks or soil by natural forces, such as water and wind

**grasslands** large, open areas of land where grass grows

**Great Plains** a large, grassland region of central North America

**nutrients** vitamins, minerals, and other substances needed by living things for health and growth

**restored** repaired, cleaned, or returned to the original condition

**settlers** people who live and make a home in a new place

# Read More

**Berglund, Bruce.** *The Black Sunday Dust Blizzard: A Day That Changed America (Days That Changed America).* North Mankato, MN: Capstone Press, 2023.

**Kenney, Karen Latchana.** *The Great Depression (U.S. History: Need to Know).* Minneapolis: Bearport Publishing, 2024.

**Klatte, Kathleen A.** *Droughts (Rosen Verified: Natural Disasters).* Buffalo, NY: Rosen Publishing, 2023.

# Learn More Online

1. Go to **www.factsurfer.com** or scan the QR code below.
2. Enter **"Dust Bowl"** into the search box.
3. Click on the cover of this book to see a list of websites.

# Index

**Black Sunday** 4

**crops** 7–10, 12, 16, 18, 20, 24

**drought** 12, 16, 18, 24, 26

**dust storms** 4, 14, 26

**economy** 16

**grasslands** 6, 8, 12, 22, 26, 28

**Great Depression** 16

**Great Plains** 4, 6, 9, 12

**Homestead Act** 6

**New Deal** 20, 22

**nutrients** 8–9, 22

**President Roosevelt, Franklin D.** 20–21

**settlers** 6–10

**trees** 12, 22–23

**wheat** 10, 16, 24

# About the Author

Karen Latchana Kenney is an author in Minnetonka, MN. She has written many books about nature and the environment.